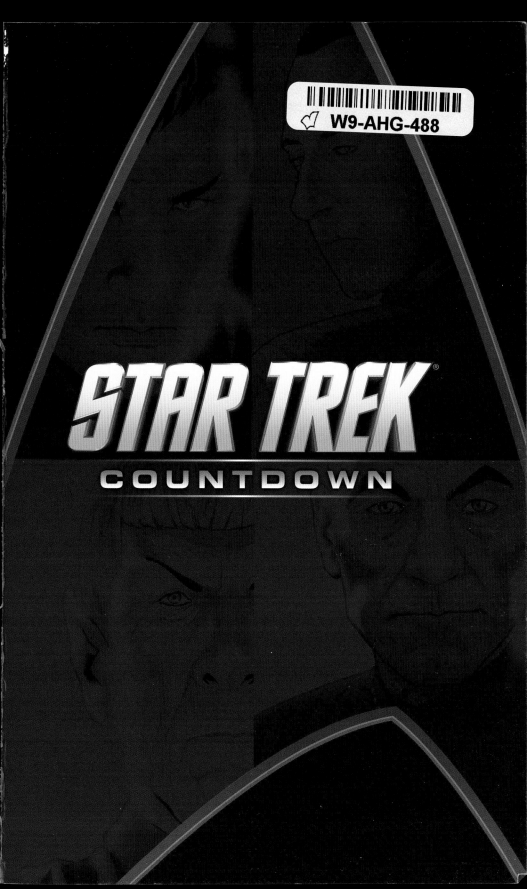

# STAR TREK

## COUNTDOWN

# STAR TREK
## COUNTDOWN

STORY
### ROBERTO ORCI & ALEX KURTZMAN

WRITERS
### MIKE JOHNSON & TIM JONES

ARTIST
### DAVID MESSINA

COLOR ART
### GIOVANNA NIRO

ADDITIONAL COLORS
### DAVID MESSINA AND PAOLO MADDALENI

COLOR CONSULTANT
### ILARIA TRAVERSI

LETTERERS
### CHRIS MOWRY, ROBERT ROBBINS, AND NEIL UYETAKE

CREATIVE CONSULTANT
### DAVID BARONOFF

ORIGINAL SERIES EDITORS
### ANDY SCHMIDT AND SCOTT DUNBIER

COLLECTION EDITOR
### JUSTIN EISINGER

COLLECTION DESIGNER
### NEIL UYETAKE

www.IDWPUBLISHING.com
ISBN: 978-1-60010-642-2    12 11 10 09    1 2 2 4

IDW Publishing
Operations:
Ted Adams, Chief Executive Officer
Greg Goldstein, Chief Operating Officer
Matthew Ruzicka, CPA, Chief Financial Officer
Alan Payne, VP of Sales
Lorelei Bunjes, Dir. of Digital Services
AnnaMaria White, Marketing & PR Manager
Marci Hubbard, Executive Assistant
Alonzo Simon, Shipping Manager
Angela Loggins, Staff Accountant
Editorial:
Chris Ryall, Publisher/Editor-in-Chief
Scott Dunbier, Editor, Special Projects
Andy Schmidt, Senior Editor
Justin Eisinger, Editor
Kris Oprisko, Editor/Foreign Lic.
Denton J. Tipton, Editor
Tom Waltz, Editor
Mariah Huehner, Associate Editor
Carlos Guzman, Editorial Assistant
Design:
Robbie Robbins, EVP/Sr. Graphic Artist
Neil Uyetake, Art Director
Chris Mowry, Graphic Artist
Amauri Osorio, Graphic Artist
Gilberto Lazcano, Production Assistant

### STAR TREK created by Gene Roddenberry

Special Thanks to Risa Kessler and John Van Citters at CBS Consumer Products, JJ Abrams and Bryan Burk at Bad Robot Productions, Mandy Safavi, Ben Kim, Pete Chiarelli, Kim Cavyan, Steven Puri and Rafael Ruthchild at K/O Productions, and Elena Casagrande, Andrew Steven Harris, Rick Sternbach and Scott Tipton for their invaluable assistance. Additionally, David Messina would like to thank his girlfriend Sara for all her love and support.

STARDATE 64333.4

DEEP IN ROMULAN
TERRITORY...

WHERE ONLY A FEW HAVE
GONE BEFORE...

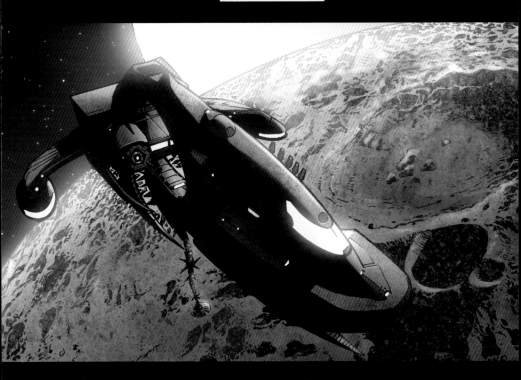

# STAR TREK

## COUNTDOWN
### NUMBER ONE

ROMULUS.

MY **HOME** FOR THE LAST TWENTY YEARS.

CURIOSITY, TOLERANCE, AND DIPLOMACY CEASED TO BE FORBIDDEN WORDS IN THE EMPIRE.

I BELIEVE THAT ONCE THE STAR GOES SUPERNOVA, IT WILL THREATEN TO DEVOUR NOT ONLY THE NEARBY SYSTEMS...

...BUT THE *ENTIRE ROMULAN EMPIRE*.

I URGE YOU TO VERIFY THE RESULTS OF MY STUDY. BUT MORE IMPORTANTLY, I BELIEVE I HAVE A *SOLUTION*.

PREPOSTEROUS!

HOW CAN *ONE STAR* DESTROY AN *EMPIRE*?

THE RARE ISOTOPE DECALITHIUM CAN BE PROCESSED TO CREATE HIGHLY VOLATILE "RED MATTER." WITH THE RIGHT AMOUNT OF RED MATTER, WE CAN CREATE AN ARTIFICIAL BLACK HOLE THAT WILL DEVOUR THE HOBUS SUPERNOVA BEFORE IT CAN SPREAD.

AND WHERE DO YOU EXPECT TO FIND THE TECHNOLOGY FOR *THAT*?

VULCAN.

ORDER! ORDER!

THIS IS ALL A *VULCAN PLOT!*

VULCAN?!

BOOO!

OUTRAGEOUS!

AMBASSADOR SPOCK, PLEASE FORGIVE THE RUDENESS OF MY COLLEAGUES.

BUT I ASSURE YOU THAT THE BEST SCIENTIFIC MINDS ON ROMULUS HAVE STUDIED THE HOBUS STAR AND HAVE *NOT* COME TO THE SAME CATACLYSMIC CONCLUSIONS.

AND DECALITHIUM IS A RARE AND VALUABLE RAW MATERIAL IN THE EMPIRE. WE WILL NOT WILLINGLY HAND IT OVER TO THE VULCANS, DESPITE YOUR WELL-INTENTIONED SUPPLICATIONS.

POINT OF ORDER!

15

I'LL BE BACK AS SOON AS I CAN.

I WON'T MISS THE BIRTH OF OUR CHILD. I *PROMISE*.

PROMISE ME YOU WON'T COME BACK UNTIL YOU'VE *SUCCEEDED*. OUR SON WOULDN'T WANT ANY LESS.

OUR—?

YES, MY LOVE. OUR *SON*. AND YES, HE WILL BE A MINER LIKE HIS FATHER.

NOW GO, AND MAKE US BOTH PROUD.

YES, MY LOVE.

MY LOVE...

KROOOOM
KROOOOM

THAT'S A *FEDERATION* SHIP!

NOT JUST ANY SHIP. AND NOT JUST ANY CAPTAIN.

STARDATE 64390.1

DEEPER IN ROMULAN
TERRITORY...

WHERE ONLY A FEW HAVE
GONE BEFORE...

# STAR TREK
## COUNTDOWN
### NUMBER TWO

CAPTAIN, SCANS PICKING UP CHARGED WEAPONS AT THE TARGET'S LOCATION!

INTERESTING.

LOCK ONTO THE WEAPONS' SIGNATURES AND BEAM THEM AWAY.

WHAT'S HAPP—

RRAAH!

KRNCH

"NICE OF THE ENTERPRISE TO HELP US WITH REPAIRS."

"BUT DOES THE CREW TRUST THEM?"

"YES, I THINK FOR THE MOST PART THEY DO. IT HELPS THAT THEY OFFERED TO REPAIR OUR SHIP AND ESCORT US TO VULCAN."

BUT DO *YOU* TRUST THEM, AYEL?

FOR THE MOST PART. WILL YOU ACCEPT THEIR INVITATION TO TRAVEL TO VULCAN ABOARD THEIR SHIP?

I HAVE BEEN PROMISED FULL ACCESS TO THE SHIP AS A SHOW OF GOODWILL.

WILL IT BE WORTH IT, NERO?

"THAT DEPENDS ON WHAT THEY MEAN BY 'FULL ACCESS.' FIRST A TOUR, NO DOUBT, WHICH WILL BE FUN...

"...THEN, THE POLITE DINNER WHERE THEY ATTEMPT TO PREPARE ROMULAN DISHES."

"MAYBE SPOCK WILL COOK."

"OH, I'D BETTER TAKE OVER SOME ROMULAN ALE. YOU KNOW HOW THEY ARE ABOUT ROMULAN ALE."

"NO DOUBT THERE WILL BE SOME FORM OF AFTER DINNER ENTERTAINMENT."

"FINALLY, I WILL RETURN TO MY LUXURIOUS SUITE...

"...AND MINE THE SHIP'S DATABASE FOR ALL IT'S WORTH.

| Hobus system | ACCESS DENIED |
| Red Matter | ACCESS DENIED |
| Decalithium | ACCESS DENIED |
| Memory-Alpha | ACCESS DENIED |

SHOCKING...

"HOPEFULLY, I CAN LEARN SOMETHING USEFUL."

| Starfleet | ACCESS GRANTED |
| History | ACCESS GRANTED |
| Enterprise | ACCESS GRANTED |
| Captains | ACCESS GRANTED |

JAMES TIBERIUS KIRK...

THANK YOU FOR JOINING ME AT THIS LATE HOUR.

NOT AT ALL. I MUST SAY YOUR NEW COMMISSION SUITS YOU WELL. WE HAVEN'T SEEN EACH OTHER SINCE BEFORE YOUR... HOW SHALL I PUT IT...

...RESURRECTION?

ACTUALLY, "RESURRECTION" CARRIES WITH IT RELIGIOUS CONNOTATIONS NOT APPLICABLE TO MY SITUATION. A MORE APT DESCRIPTION WOULD BE A SIMPLE "RETURN," DENOTING THE FACT THAT MY NEURAL NETS WERE SUCCESSFULLY IMPRINTED ONTO B-4'S EXISTING PROGRAMMING.

YOU AND I SHARE A UNIQUE EXPERIENCE. BUT SOMETHING TELLS ME THAT YOU DISTURBED THIS OLD HALF-VULCAN'S SLEEP FOR SOMETHING ELSE.

INDEED. I RECEIVED A STARFLEET COMMAND COMMUNIQUÉ REGARDING THE HOBUS PHENOMENA.

THE FEDERATION HAS AUTHORIZED A COVERT OPERATION TO THE HOBUS SYSTEM TO DRILL DIRECTLY INTO THE STAR TO PREVENT IT FROM GOING NOVA.

A COVERT FEDERATION MISSION INTO ROMULAN SPACE?

"I FEAR OUR SITUATION HAS BECOME MUCH MORE COMPLICATED..."

VRRRMMM

GREETINGS, *AMBASSADOR.* YOU WILL FORGIVE ME IF I AM NOT INCLINED TO OFFER YOU THE GREETING CUSTOM WOULD DICTATE FOR A RETURNING SON OF VULCAN.

AND YOUR LACK OF FALSE PRETENSES IS APPRECIATED, PRAETOR. I AM AWARE OF MY REPUTATION IN THE SENATE.

NOT JUST THE SENATE, SPOCK. *THE WHOLE OF VULCAN.*

YOU ONCE BROUGHT GREAT GLORY TO OUR PLANET. BUT YOUR DECISION TO FORSAKE YOUR HERITAGE, TO SPEND SO MANY YEARS DEEP IN THE BOSOM OF OUR GREATEST ENEMY, HAS TARNISHED YOUR NAME.

WHEN YOU DECIDED TO LIVE ON ROMULUS, YOU LEFT ONLY MISTRUST AND SUSPICION BEHIND YOU.

A SITUATION OF WHICH I WAS FULLY AWARE WHEN I UNDERTOOK MY MISSION TO ROMULUS. A MISSION OF PEACE BETWEEN EMPIRES. A PEACE THAT HAS LASTED FOR AS LONG AS I HAVE LIVED THERE.

BUT IF YOUR SUSPICION IS SO GREAT, WHY ALLOW ME HERE AT ALL?

I SUPPOSE YOU COULD CALL IT—

AND YOU MUST BE MR. NERO. SPOCK SPEAKS VERY HIGHLY OF YOU.

IT'S AN HONOR, AMBASSADOR. I READ OF YOUR DISTINGUISHED RECORD AS CAPTAIN IN THE ENTERPRISE DATABANKS.

PREPARING FOR A BATTLE AT THE TRANSPORTER BAY, WERE YOU M'KAN? YOU CAN CALL OFF THE DOGS.

I'VE ARRANGED FOR SPOCK TO ADDRESS THE SCIENCE COUNCIL AT ONCE.

TELL ME, MR. NERO, WHAT ARE YOUR FIRST IMPRESSIONS OF VULCAN?

IT'S... *SPECTACULAR*. SO DIFFERENT FROM ROMULUS, AND YET...

PERHAPS IT'S JUST THE MINER IN ME LOOKING AT ALL THIS ROCK. I CAN'T HELP FEELING SOMEWHAT AT HOME.

COME NOW... THE COUNCIL *AWAITS*.

THERE'S MORE, NERO. THE STAR IS INCREASINGLY UNSTABLE. THE ROMULAN SENATE HAS ISSUED AN *EVACUATION ORDER* FOR THE PLANET. FEDERATION SHIPS ARE EN ROUTE TO HELP, BUT TIME GROWS SHORT.

*ENOUGH! I'M LEAVING NOW!*

I'M GOING BACK TO GET MY WIFE AND CHILD BEFORE IT'S *TOO LATE!*

NERO, *WAIT!*

THERE'S STILL A *CHANCE.* LEAVE THE DECALITHIUM WITH US. AMBASSADOR PICARD AND I WILL DO WHATEVER WE MUST TO SEE OUR PLAN THROUGH.

THE FATE OF US *ALL* DEPENDS ON IT.

VERY WELL. YOU CAN KEEP THE DECALITHIUM. DO YOUR BEST.

BUT I WARN YOU, SPOCK...

IF ROMULUS DIES, I WILL HOLD *YOUR* PEOPLE RESPONSIBLE.

ROMULUS IS DEAD.

# STAR TREK
## COUNTDOWN
### NUMBER THREE

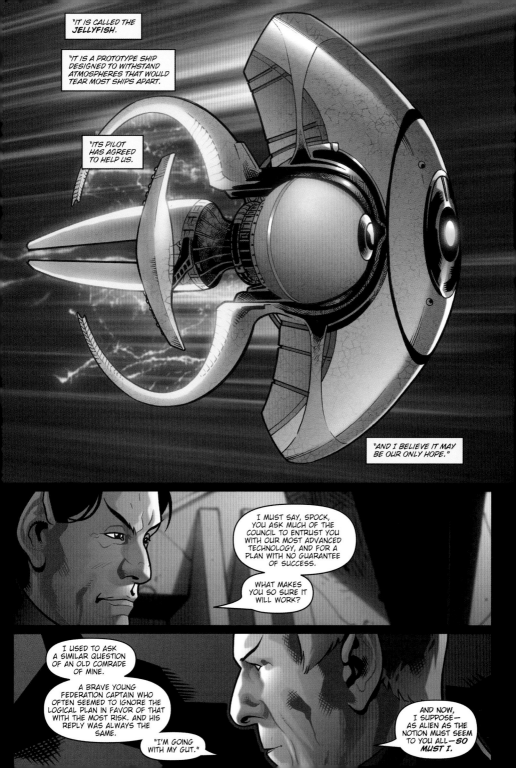

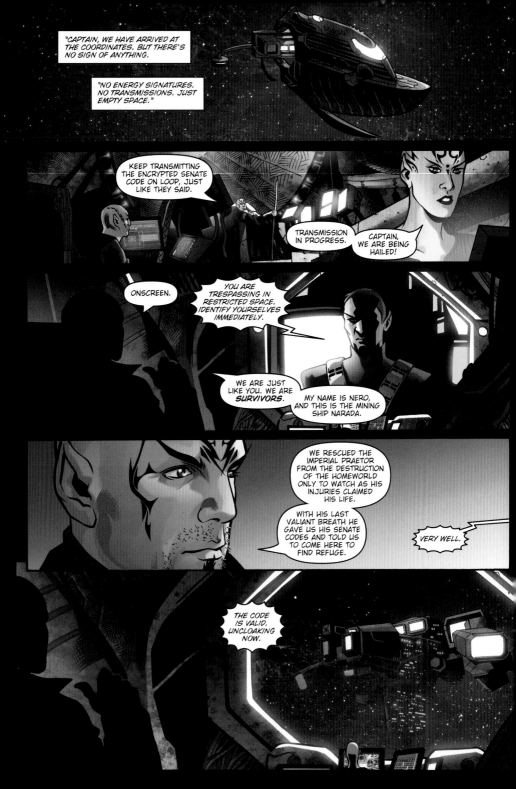

"CAPTAIN, WE HAVE ARRIVED AT THE COORDINATES. BUT THERE'S NO SIGN OF ANYTHING.

"NO ENERGY SIGNATURES. NO TRANSMISSIONS. JUST EMPTY SPACE."

KEEP TRANSMITTING THE ENCRYPTED SENATE CODE ON LOOP, JUST LIKE THEY SAID.

TRANSMISSION IN PROGRESS.

CAPTAIN, WE ARE BEING HAILED!

ONSCREEN.

YOU ARE TRESPASSING IN RESTRICTED SPACE. IDENTIFY YOURSELVES IMMEDIATELY.

WE ARE JUST LIKE YOU. WE ARE **SURVIVORS**.

MY NAME IS NERO, AND THIS IS THE MINING SHIP NARADA.

WE RESCUED THE IMPERIAL PRAETOR FROM THE DESTRUCTION OF THE HOMEWORLD ONLY TO WATCH AS HIS INJURIES CLAIMED HIS LIFE.

WITH HIS LAST VALIANT BREATH HE GAVE US HIS SENATE CODES AND TOLD US TO COME HERE TO FIND REFUGE.

VERY WELL.

THE CODE IS VALID. UNCLOAKING NOW.

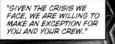

"WE ARE AN ADVANCED MILITARY FACILITY WHOSE EXISTENCE IS KNOWN ONLY TO THE ROMULAN HIGH COMMAND.

"IN THE EVENT OF A THREAT TO THE HOMEWORLD WE WERE TASKED WITH PROVIDING SAFE HAVEN FOR THE RULING COUNCIL.

"GIVEN THE CRISIS WE FACE, WE ARE WILLING TO MAKE AN EXCEPTION FOR YOU AND YOUR CREW."

WELCOME TO *THE VAULT,* CAPTAIN NERO.

I AM COMMANDER D'SPAL.

WE'VE BEEN WAITING FOR WORD FROM THE RULING COUNCIL SINCE THE HOMEWORLD WAS LOST, BUT YOU ARE THE FIRST TO REPORT ANY CONTACT WITH THEM.

WE ARE THE RENDEZVOUS POINT FOR WHAT REMAINS OF THE FLEET. SO UNTIL OUR FORCES CAN REGROUP AND RECOVER...

THIS STATION IS THE *LAST HOPE* OF THE ROMULAN EMPIRE.

VULCAN.

THE VULCAN ENGINEERS ARE MODIFYING THE JELLYFISH PER YOUR INSTRUCTIONS IN ORDER TO CARRY THE RED MATTER SAFELY.

YEAH. STILL LIKE TO DO ALL THE WORK ON HER MYSELF THOUGH, Y'KNOW?

I UNDERSTAND. I AM REMINDED OF HOW YOU WOULD OFTEN REFER TO ENGINEERING ON THE ENTERPRISE. THE JELLYFISH IS YOUR "BABY," IS SHE NOT?

AMEN, CAPTAIN. AND I FEEL LIKE I'M SENDING HER ON A SUICIDE MISSION.

YET AS BLEAK AS THE SITUATION APPEARS, I AM GLAD TO BE REUNITED WITH YOU AND AMBASSADOR PICARD.

TOGETHER WE HAVE ENCOUNTERED EQUALLY IMPOSSIBLE DILEMMAS IN THE PAST AND FOUND A SOLUTION.

YOU'RE RIGHT. LOCUTUS. LORE. DEVIDIA II. PRETTY MUCH ANY RUN IN WITH Q. AND NOW WE'VE GOT A HUNGRY STAR THAT COULD DESTROY US ALL.

JUST LIKE *OLD TIMES*, MY FRIEND.

AMBASSADOR PICARD'S QUARTERS.

MEMBERS OF THE ROMULAN HIGH COUNCIL.

THEY WERE FOUND FLOATING IN SPACE NEAR THE LAST KNOWN LOCATION OF THE FEDERATION EVACUATION GROUP THAT WE SENT TO ROMULUS.

ALONG WITH THE BODY OF THE PRAETOR, STABBED THROUGH THE HEART.

NO SIGN OF THEIR VESSEL, AND NO TRACE OF THE FEDERATION SHIPS. IT'S AS IF THEY SIMPLY DISAPPEARED.

POSSIBLY.

NERO.

IN THE PAST FEW DAYS THERE HAVE BEEN REPORTS OF MORE SHIPS VANISHING CLOSE TO ROMULAN SPACE. FEDERATION. CARDASSIAN. *EVEN KLINGON.*

BUT THE NARADA WAS A SIMPLE MINING SHIP.

INDEED. UNLESS HE FOUND *NEW* ALLIES.

69

WHEN HE LEFT HERE, HE ALL BUT THREATENED TO RETURN TO VULCAN FOR RETRIBUTION SHOULD ROMULUS BE DESTROYED.

YOU KNEW NERO BETTER THAN I, BUT THERE WAS SOMETHING ABOUT HIM THAT MADE ME INCLINED TO BELIEVE WHAT HE SAID.

WHICH MEANS I MUST DEPART IN THE JELLYFISH EVEN SOONER THAN ANTICIPATED.

YOU IN THE JELLYFISH? I THOUGHT GEORDI HAD VOLUNTEERED.

I CONVINCED HIM OTHERWISE. IT IS POTENTIALLY A ONE-WAY TRIP, AS YOU MIGHT SAY. AND HE IS STILL A YOUNG MAN.

BUT I... I AM REACHING THE END OF MY ADVENTURES.

IT WAS I WHO FIRST WARNED OF THE DANGER FROM THE HOBUS STAR. IT WAS I WHO CONVINCED NERO TO HELP ME TRY TO STOP IT. AND IT WAS I WHO FAILED TO PREDICT WHEN THE STAR WOULD GO NOVA.

I WAS THERE AT THE BEGINNING. AND I MUST BE THERE AT THE END. I ONLY PRAY THAT NERO DOES NOT CARRY OUT HIS THREAT.

I UNDERSTAND. AND I KNOW THERE IS NO POINT TRYING TO CONVINCE YOU OTHERWISE.

BUT AS FOR NERO, IF HE IS PLANNING TO SEE THROUGH ON HIS PLANS...

...I'VE MADE ARRANGEMENTS TO SEE THAT HE DOESN'T GET THE CHANCE.

"THE THREAT IS NEUTRALIZED, CAPTAIN NERO.

"THE NEW SYSTEMS ARE RESPONDING EVEN BETTER THAN PROMISED."

VERY GOOD, AYEL. COLLECT WHAT SALVAGEABLE PARTS YOU CAN AND ADD THEM TO OUR STORES.

AND THEN PREPARE FOR THE FINAL WARP TO *VULCAN.*

THE BORDER OF THE ROMULAN
AND KLINGON EMPIRES.

# STAR TREK

## COUNTDOWN

### NUMBER FOUR

"CAPTAIN, UNIDENTIFIED SHIP DECLOAKING!"

HELLO AGAIN, ENTERPRISE. AS YOU CAN SEE, GENERAL WORF IS MAKING HIMSELF AT HOME ON THE NARADA.

I DON'T SEE SPOCK WITH YOU. HE'S ON HIS WAY TO STOP THE SUPERNOVA, ISN'T HE?

YOUR *CRUSADE* ENDS *HERE*, NERO!

NO AMOUNT OF KILLING WILL BRING ROMULUS BACK! SURRENDER NOW OR WE WILL BRING THE ENTIRE WEIGHT OF THE FEDERATION FLEET DOWN ON YOU!

YOU FORGET YOURSELF, PICARD. YOU'RE NOT THE CAPTAIN ANYMORE.

*CAPTAIN DATA,* THERE IS STILL A FLICKER OF LIFE IN YOUR KLINGON FRIEND. I'LL BE HAPPY TO SEND HIM BACK TO YOU. ALL YOU NEED TO DO IS LOWER YOUR SHIELDS. NERO *OUT.*

IF WE LOWER OUR SHIELDS HE WILL MOST CERTAINLY ATTEMPT TO DESTROY US.

AND WE CANNOT KNOW FOR CERTAIN THAT NERO WILL SEND WORF EVEN IF WE DO. BUT IF WE DO NOT, WORF WILL MOST CERTAINLY DIE.

NERO'S SHIELDS WILL BE DOWN AS WELL. THIS MAY BE OUR ONLY CHANCE TO STOP HIM.

IF WE CAN RESTORE SHIELDS FAST ENOUGH, DAMAGE TO THE ENTERPRISE MIGHT BE CONTAINED...

...BUT THE DECISION IS YOURS, *CAPTAIN.*

THIS IS THE FINAL FLIGHT OF THE JELLYFISH.

IN MY DISCUSSIONS WITH AMBASSADOR PICARD I OVERESTIMATED MY CHANCES FOR SURVIVAL. IT WILL BE **IMPOSSIBLE** TO ESCAPE THE PULL OF THE SINGULARITY I HOPE TO CREATE.

THIS BROADCAST MAY NEVER BE RECEIVED, BUT IN THE EVENT THAT IT IS, PLEASE DELIVER IT TO THE SCIENCE ACADEMY ON VULCAN THAT IT MAY BE INCLUDED IN THE ARCHIVES.

THE RED MATTER CONTAINMENT AND DELIVERY SYSTEMS WORKED PERFECTLY.

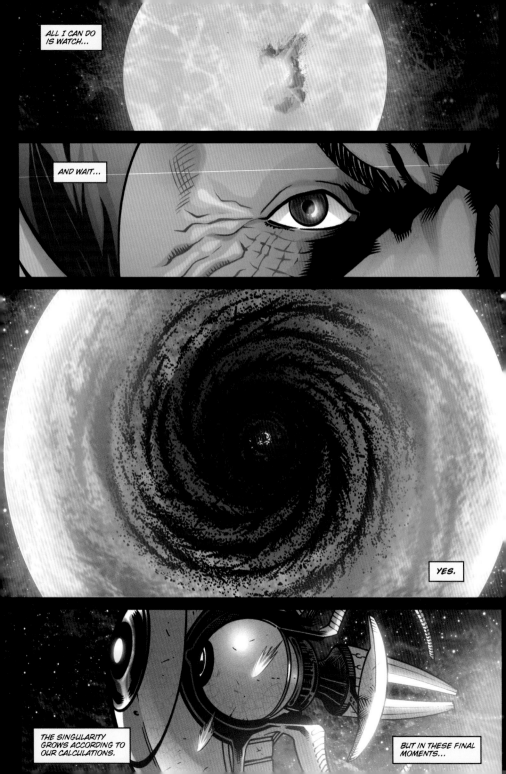

SPOCK!

I WILL HAVE MY VENGEANCE!!

I WILL HAVE—

IT IS DONE.

THE HOBUS STAR IS NO LONGER A THREAT TO THE GALAXY.

BUT I AM TRAPPED BY THE SINGULARITY NOW.

TO MY FRIENDS WHO MIGHT HEAR THIS MESSAGE, DO NOT GRIEVE. IT IS ONLY LOGICAL.

THE NEEDS OF THE MANY OUTW—

# AFTERWORD

The notion that we'd be called to serve *STAR TREK* in any form is something we never dared dream. This book has had particular meaning for us in that we fell in love with *STAR TREK* through the characters of *THE NEXT GENERATION*. The longest summer of our lives was spent waiting to find out how Captain Riker and the amazing crew of the Enterprise were going to defeat their former Captain, Jean-Luc Picard, after his transformation into Locutus of Borg.

We don't expect to ever feel the same anticipation again, but perhaps we can create some for new fans. That is the intention of this book... to take a ride with a beloved crew that no one believed could ever match the original, and to pay homage to their stewardship of a thing called *STAR TREK*. Their journey now takes us back to the beginning...

Roberto Orci & Alex Kurtzman

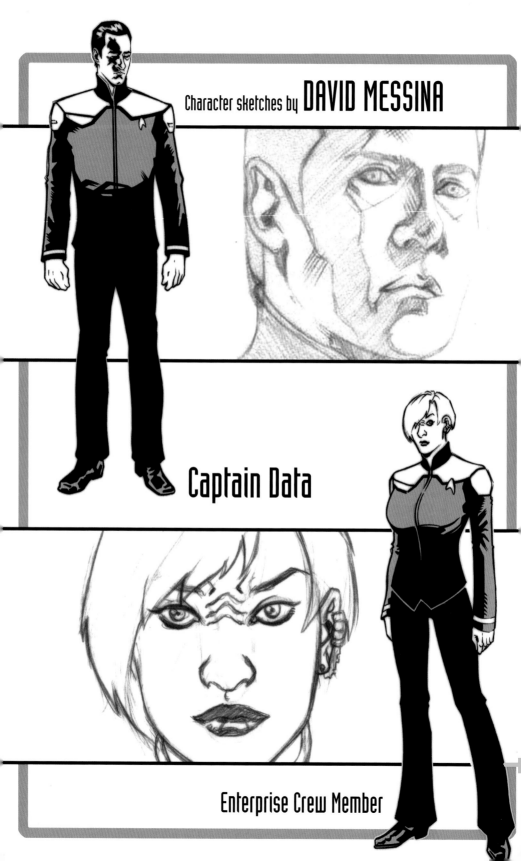

Character sketches by **DAVID MESSINA**

Captain Data

Enterprise Crew Member

Enterprise Crew Member

Enterprise Crew Member

Nero
on Romulus

Nero
post Romulus

# Ambassador Spock

Captain Data and Enterprise Crew